my first picture dictionary

drawings by Gillian Chapman

Dolphin Publications

Aa

asleep

arch

ant

alphabet

apple

afraid

alligator

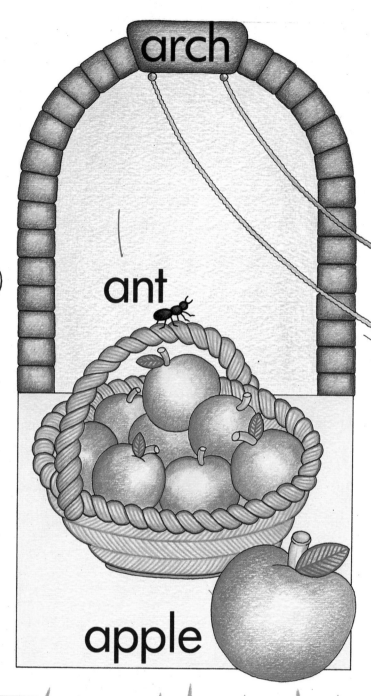

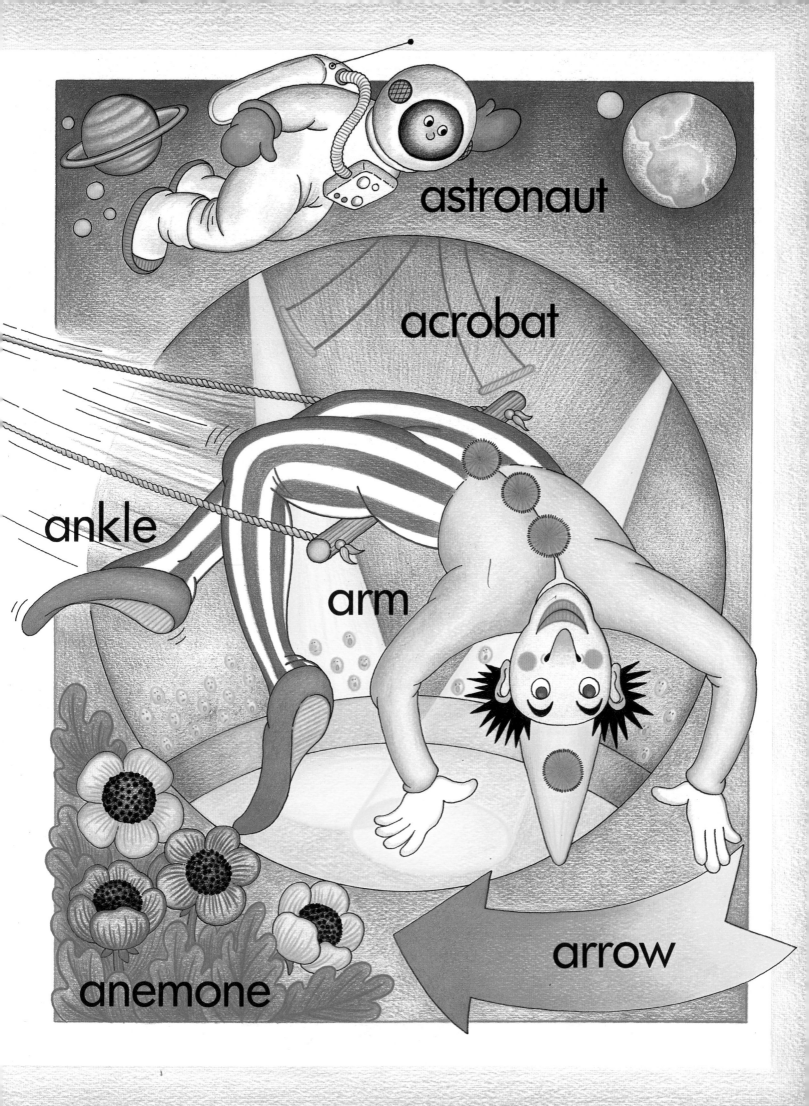

astronaut

acrobat

ankle

arm

anemone

arrow

Aa

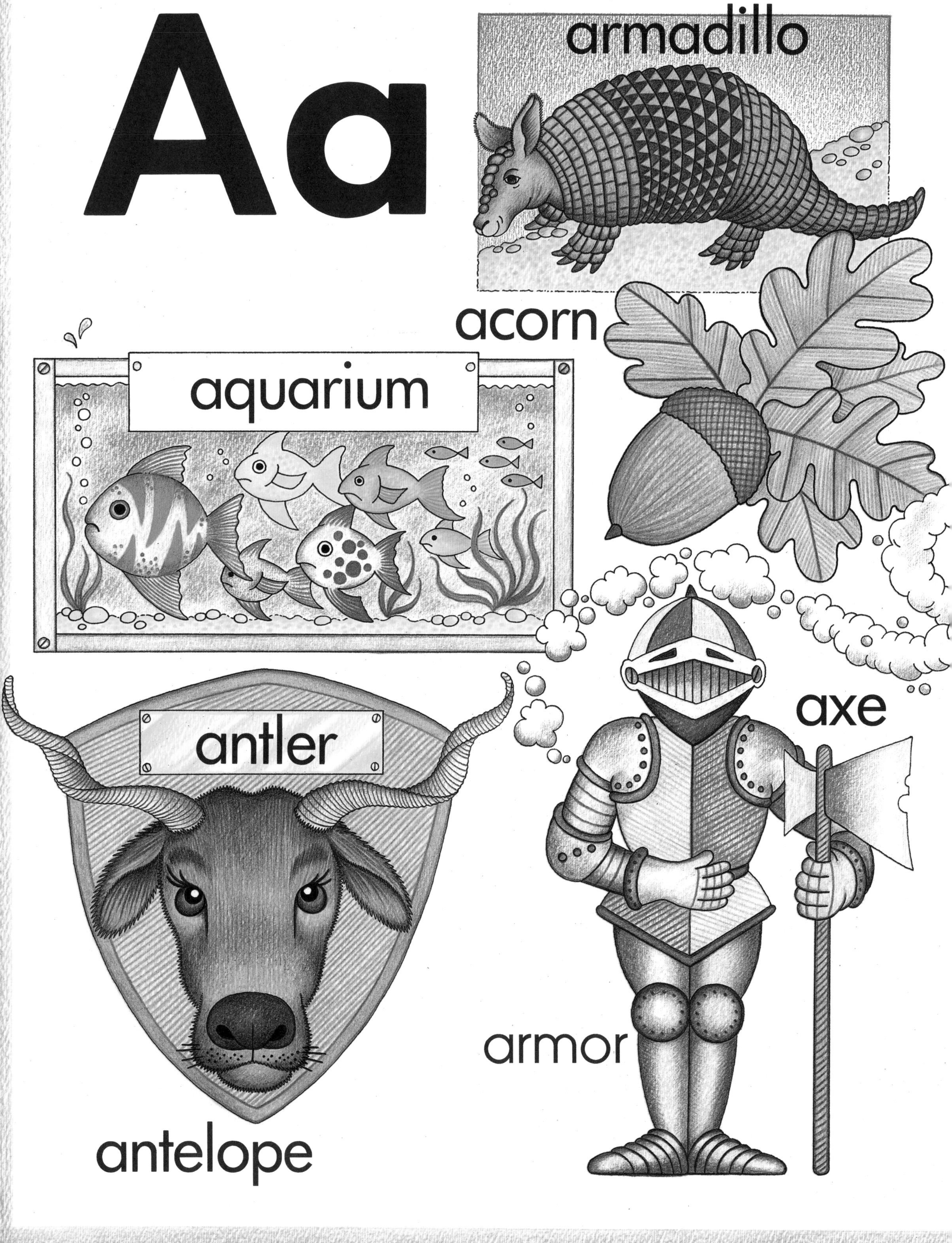

armadillo

acorn

aquarium

antler

axe

antelope

armor

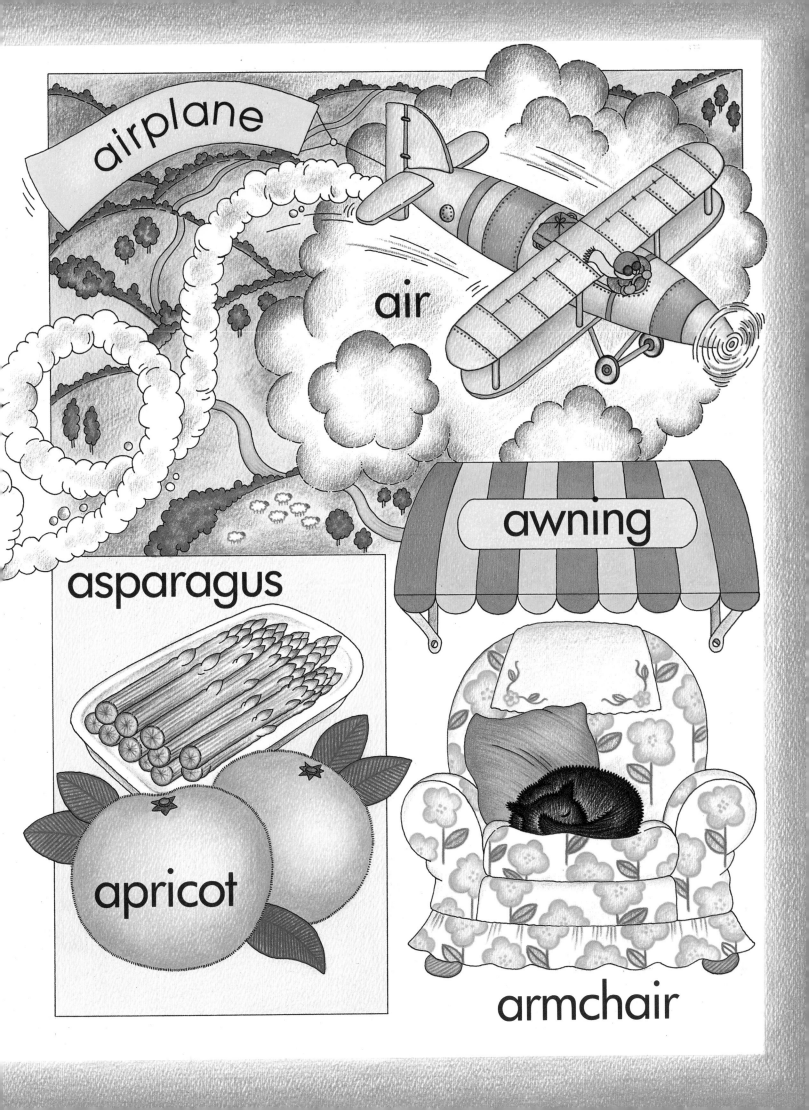

airplane

air

awning

asparagus

apricot

armchair

B b

bald

beard

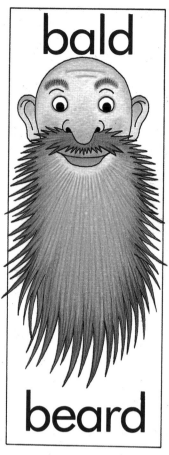

brush

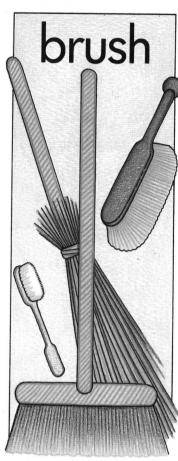

barrow

button

belt

burglar

bubbles

bath

bell

B b

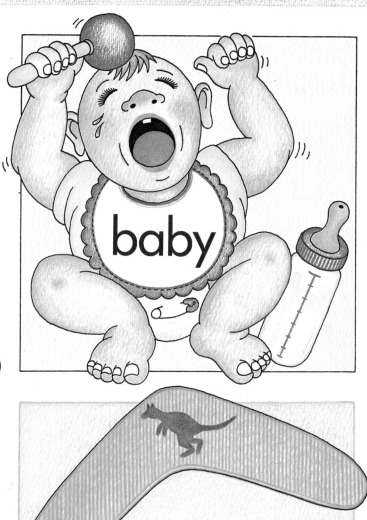
baby

breakfast

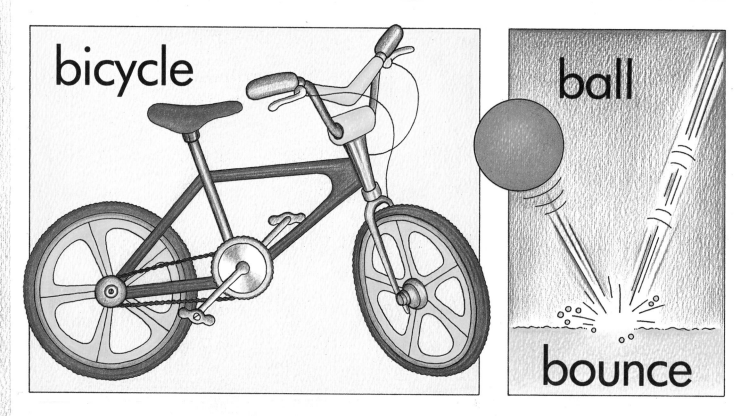

boomerang

bicycle

ball

bounce

bull

bush

bandage

blanket

bed

boots

blackberry

beetle

badger

buttercup

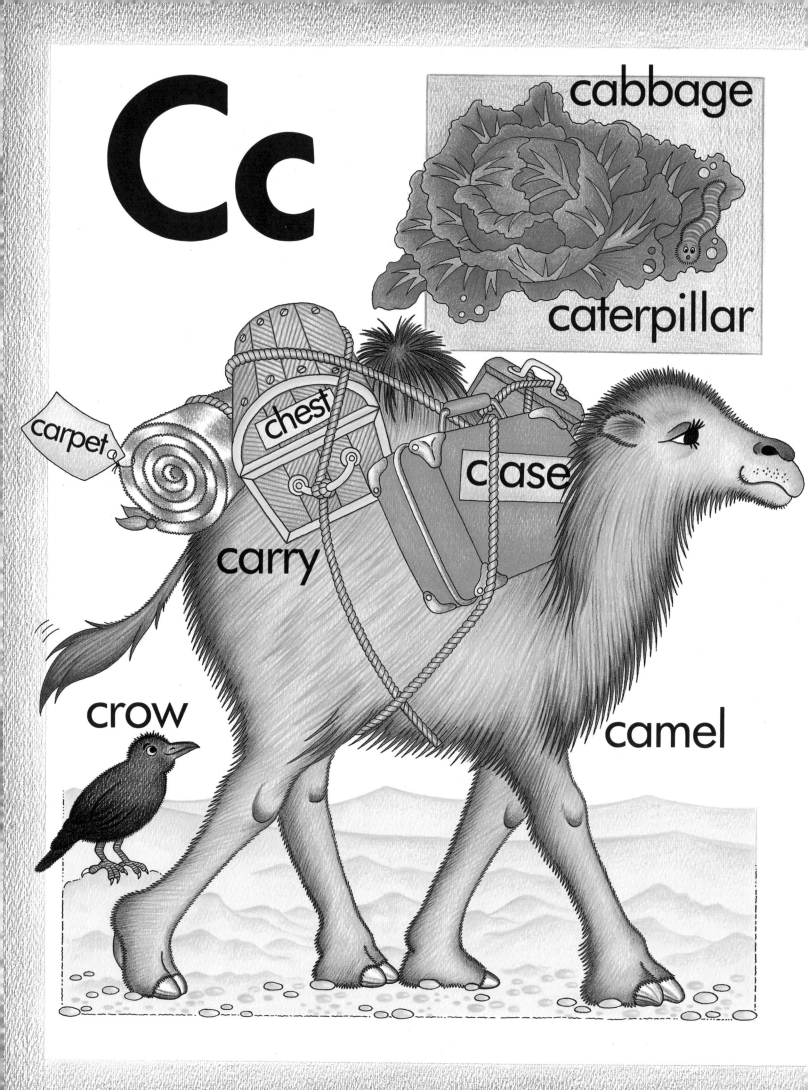

Cc

cabbage

caterpillar

carpet

chest

case

carry

crow

camel

Cc

cage

chimpanzee

cold

cat

chocolate

candle

crab

chain

Dd

drum

daisy

donkey

dirty

dog

draw

dig

drawing

deep

dragonfly

dove

dolphin

diver

dinosaur

desert

Dd

drip

dish

drink

dinner

duck

daffodil

doctor

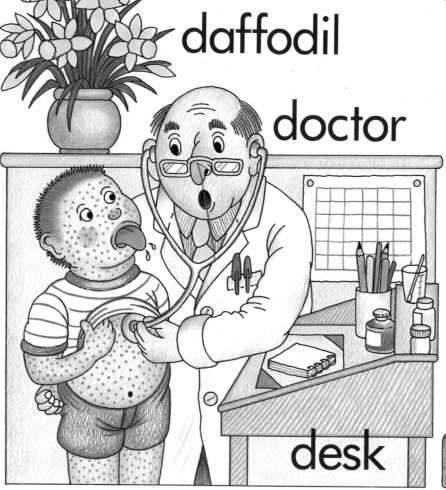

desk

door

Ee

eagle

easel

eel

eat

elbow

eight eggs

explosion

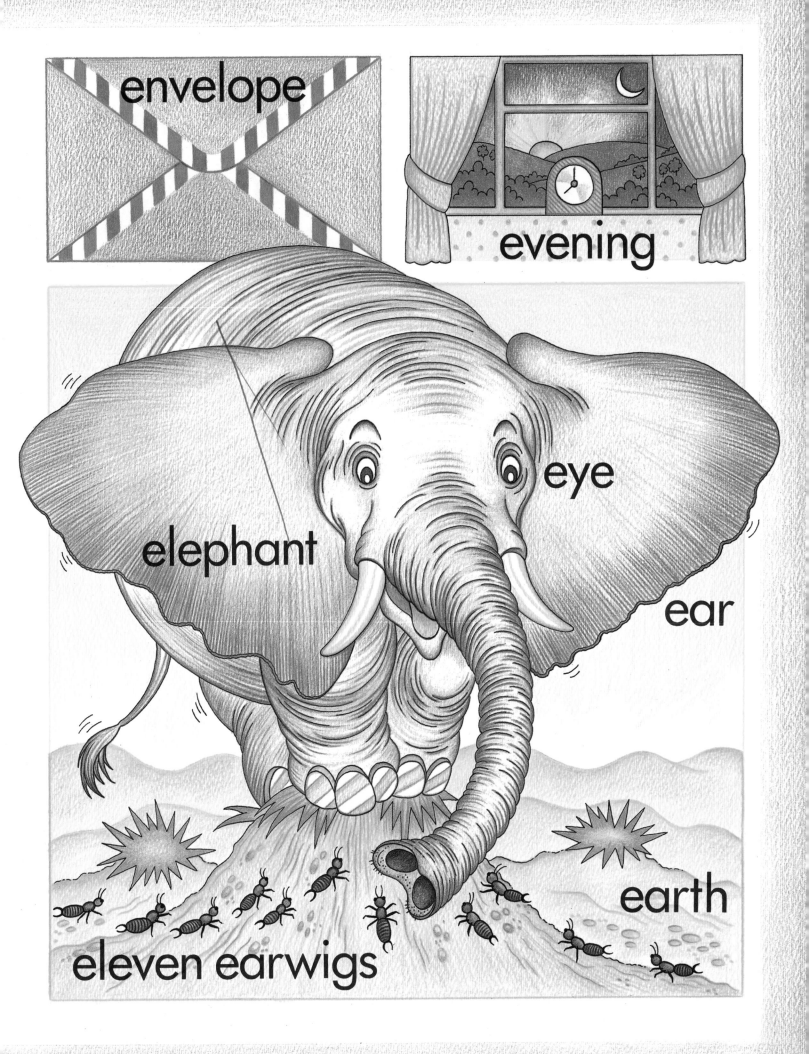

Ff

face

funny

fruit

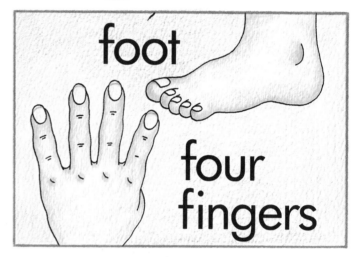

foot

four
fingers

feather

fan

flame

flamingo

fish

fire

G g

gingerbread

greedy gorilla

glue

garden

gnome

gate

grass

glass

ghost

gravy

girl

green

gloves

giraffe

gray

goal

Hh

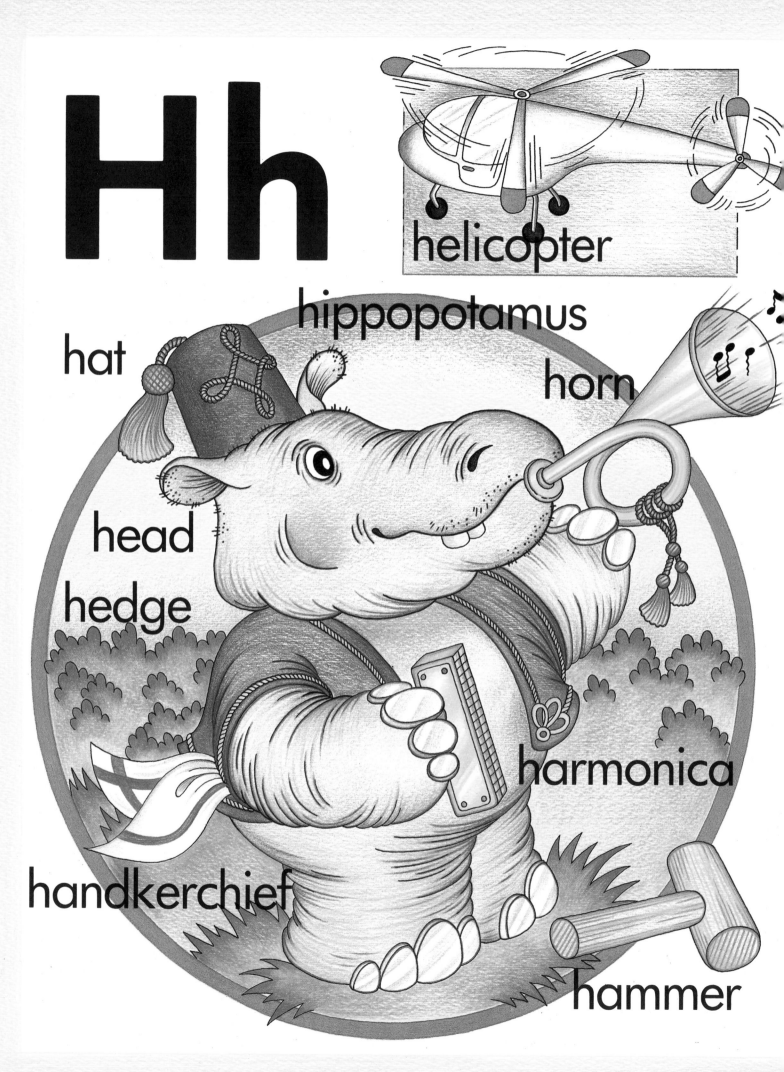

helicopter

hippopotamus

hat

horn

head

hedge

harmonica

handkerchief

hammer

Hh

hill

house

hive

hut

honey

hold

hoop

hop

hamburger

Ii

icicle

iceberg

ice cream

igloo

ice

island

icing

iron

insect

ink

Jj

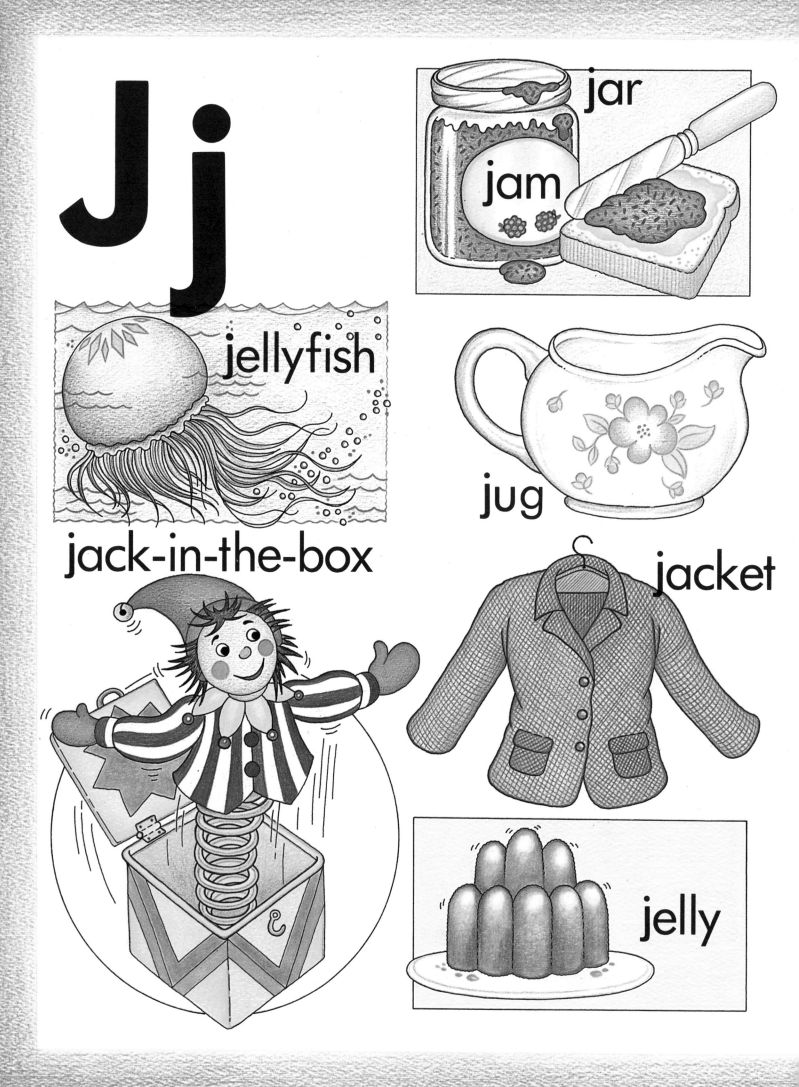

jar

jam

jellyfish

jug

jack-in-the-box

jacket

jelly

K k

kookaburra

key

koala

kilt

kangaroo

knee

kennel

kite

knock

knob

knitting

knot

kitten

kitchen

knife

kettle

L l

lamp

light

lightning

leak

lion

leopard

lick

lollipop

leg

log

leaf

lemon

lime

lobster

ladder

luggage

label

M m

mask

mouth

mirror

medicine

map

milkshake

milk

mitten

mole

mud

mop

messy

moon

mountain

moth

magician

mustache

mice

medal

mouse

magic

marigold

money

matches

money box

N n

newt

nib

net

nine

napkin

noodles

notebook

numbers

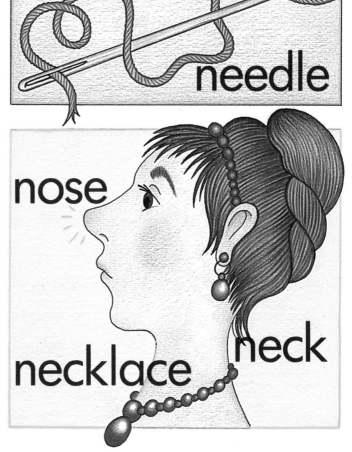
needle

nose

necklace

neck

newspaper

night

night cap

night shirt

nest

nail

notice-board

nuts

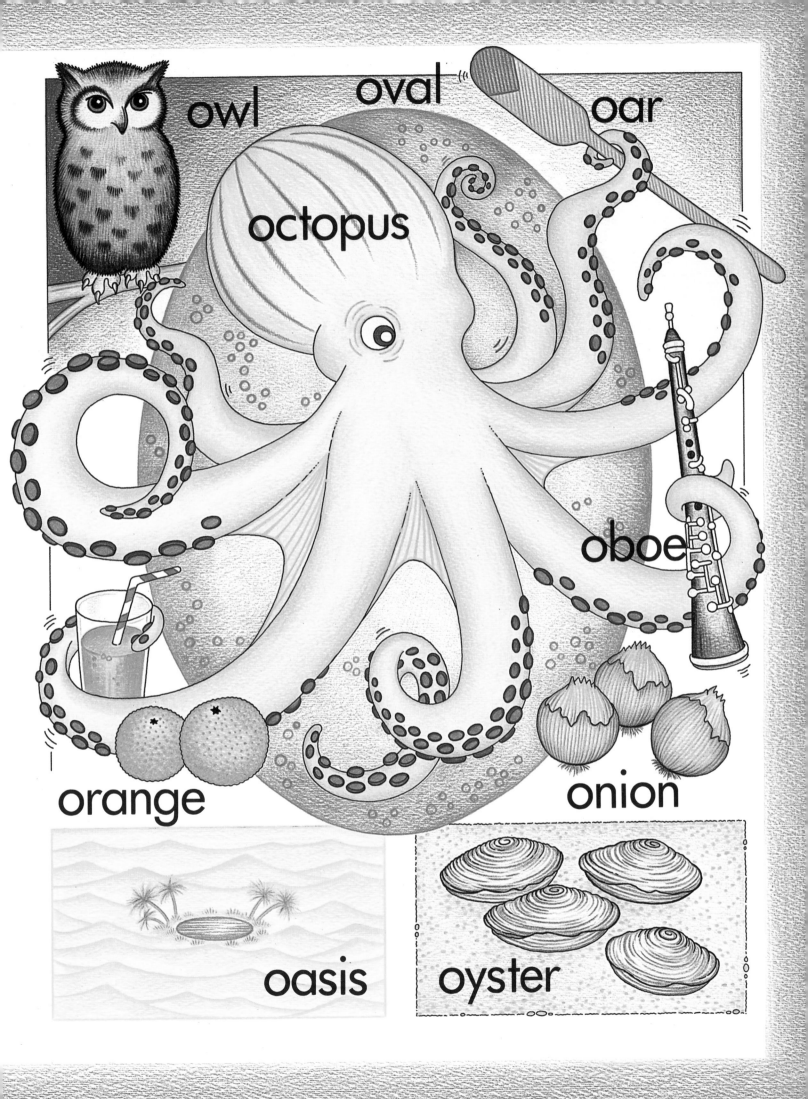

owl

oval

oar

octopus

oboe

orange

onion

oasis

oyster

P p

present

puffin

pirate

pipe

patch

post

pocket

pearls

pie peas

plate potato

pond

pigeon

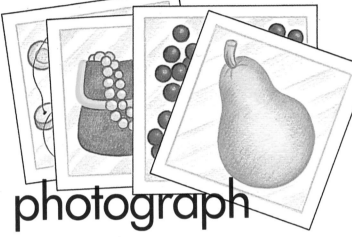

photograph

puppet

plum

pear

pineapple

Pp

parrot

palm

point

panda

picture

pig

pencil

pen

pancake

piano

parcel

puppy

painter

path

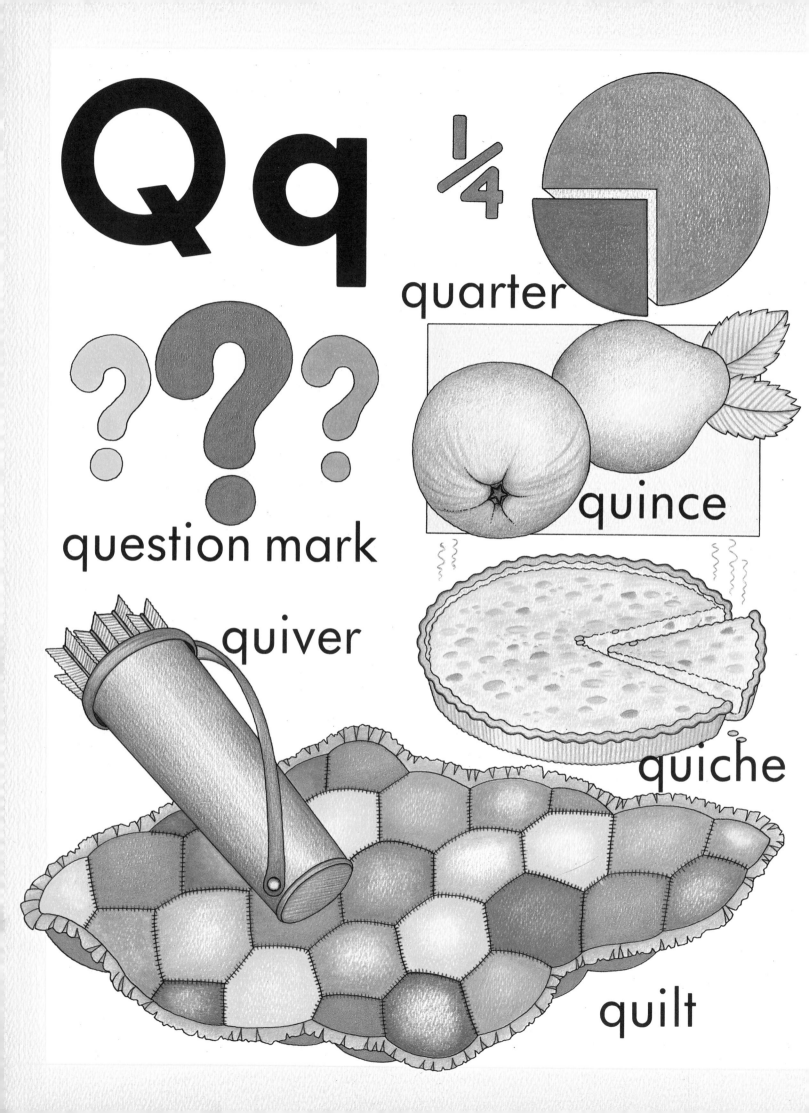

Q q ¼

quarter

question mark

quince

quiver

quiche

quilt

queen

quill

quail

Rr

rocket

rabbit

rocking-horse

radio

roller-skates

ruler

Recipe

rolling pin

ram

Ss

snake

spider

strawberry

spoon

splash!

sea

snow

snail

snowman

sock

shoe

star

sky

spaceship

S s

stamps

S. Smith
1 South Street

scissors
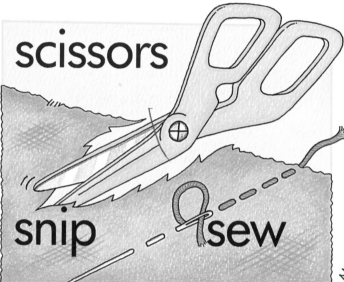
snip   sew

snowdrops

spaghetti

scarf

swan

shadow

swim

shell

starfish

smoke

smell

smile

squirrel

slippers

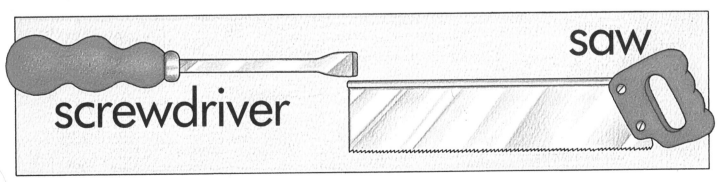

screwdriver

saw

T t

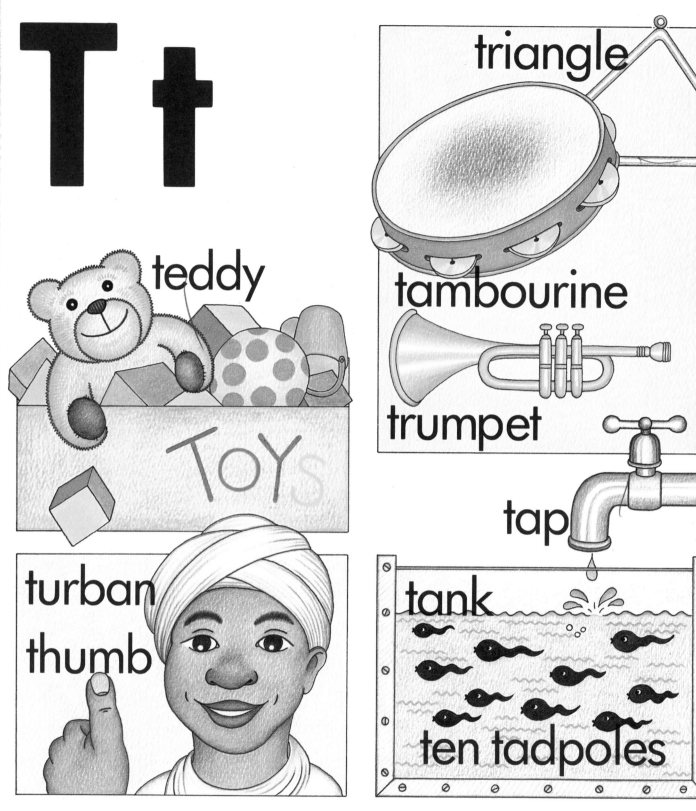

triangle

teddy

tambourine

trumpet

tap

TOYS

turban

thumb

tank

ten tadpoles

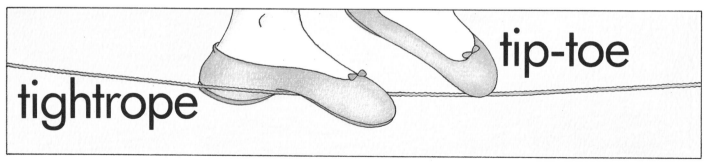

tip-toe

tightrope

T t

tunnel

ticket

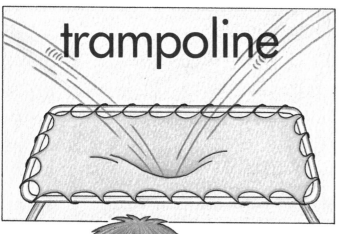
trampoline

television

teeth

tart

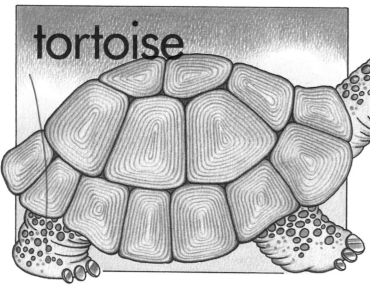
tortoise

thistle

track

train

toad

tie

tower

tallest

taller

tall

tiny

three trees

twig

teepee

U u

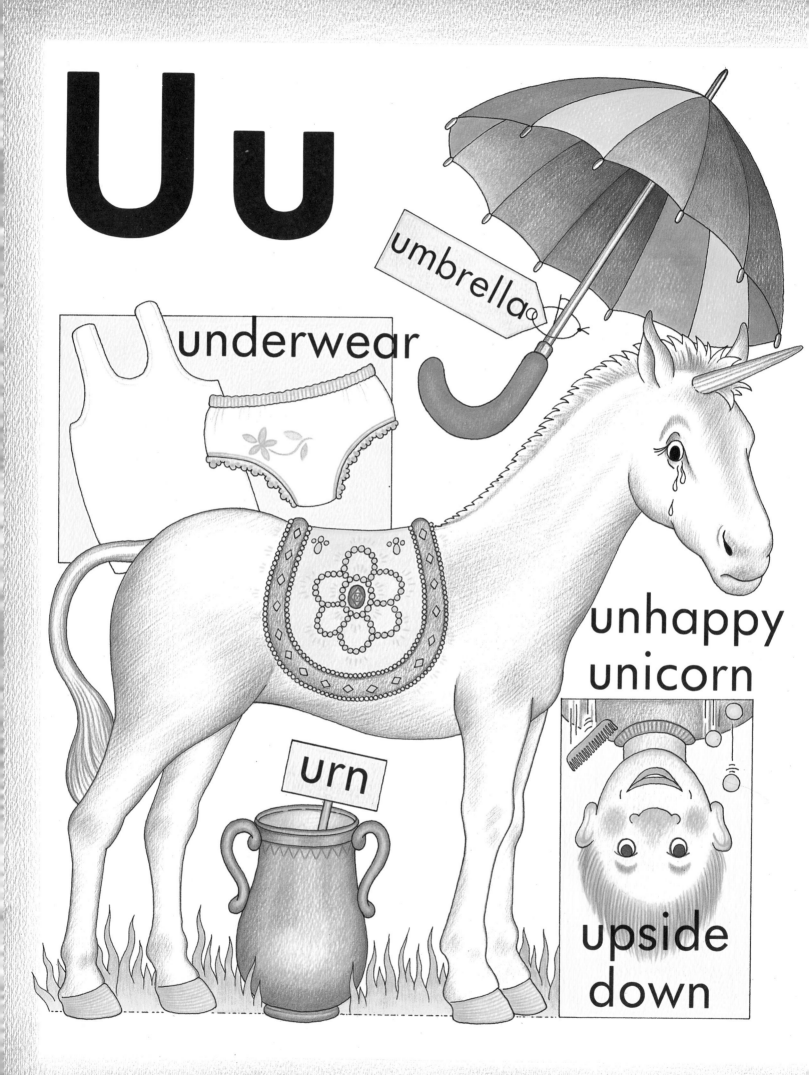

umbrella

underwear

unhappy
unicorn

urn

upside
down

V v

vulture

vegetables

valley

volcano

violin

violets

vase

Ww

washing machine

wool

woodpecker

wasp

window

wristwatch

walrus

whistle

water

wet

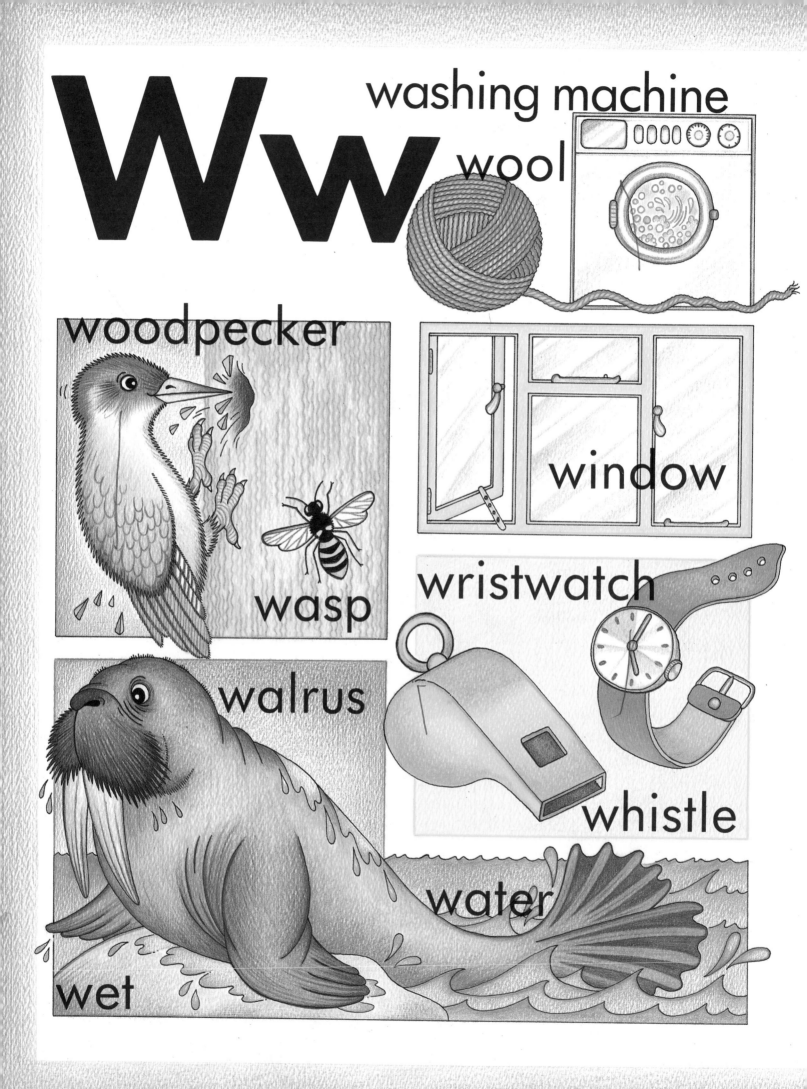

web

wand

witch

windmill

wind

wolf

whiskers

weeds

X Y Z

X-ray

xylophone

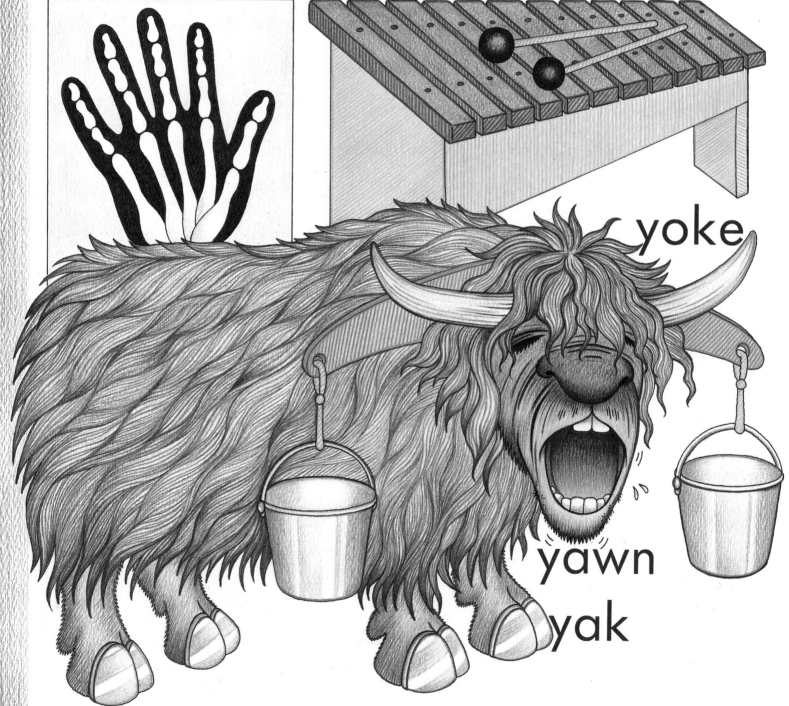

yoke

yawn

yak